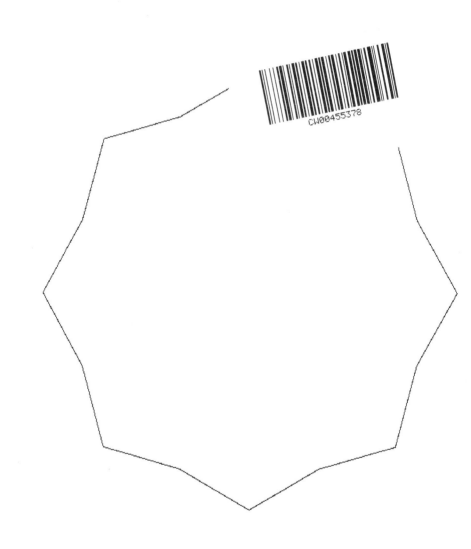

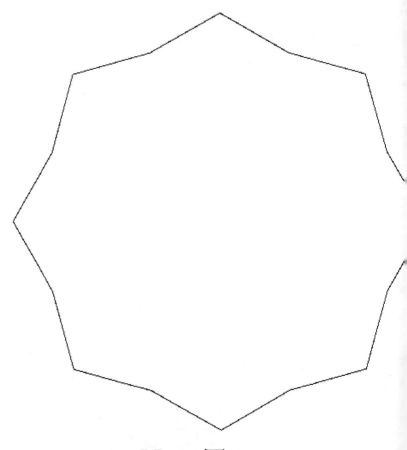

How To
Win Hearts
&
Influence Minds

Disclaimer:

This is a work of fiction. Names, characters, plac, and incidents either are the product of the author's imagination or are used factiously. Any resemblance to actual persons, living or dead, events, or locates is entirely coincidental.

Edition:

First Edition
First Edition: July 2023
This paperback edition first published in 2023

Preface

We cordially invite you to "How to Win Hearts and Influence Minds", a book that explores the fascinating realm of persuasion and its transforming potential. You will embark on a journey via these pages that mix the craft of storytelling with the rules of influence to examine how people can have a significant impact on the world around them. The idea of influence has captivated people for ages. We are continually affected by powerful people, from the great leaders who built nations to the daily heroes who inspire change in their communities. But what actually exists behind influence's apparent surface? What techniques, tactics, and subtleties enable certain people to perfect this skill and bring about long-lasting change?

The goal of "How to Win Hearts and Influence Minds" is to solve these puzzles and provide readers a thorough understanding of the ideas and methods that support persuasive behavior. We will follow the journey of our protagonist, Alex, as they navigate the complexity of influence, overcome obstacles, and realize their ultimate potential via the power of narrative. We will examine several facets of influence, such as self-awareness, empathy, communication, persuasion, leadership, and ethics, across the chapters. Through Alex's experiences and interactions with various people who have perfected the art of influencing in their own particular ways, each chapter will not only provide theoretical concepts but also explain how they can be applied practically.

This book explores more than just methods and techniques. It explores the significance of authenticity, integrity, and the moral use of power as it goes deeper into the facets of influence. It challenges readers to think about the power they have and how their decisions can have a beneficial effect that goes far beyond their immediate environment. Although "How to Win Friends and Influence Minds" is fiction, it is inspired by true accounts of important people who have had a lasting impact on culture. It combines their knowledge and insights with fictional stories to offer readers useful advice, thought-provoking reflections, and doable suggestions for improving their own persuasiveness. You are invited to join me on this immersive adventure, where you will see how our protagonist changes and learn the ideas and methods that can make you a powerful person in your own right. This book gives a roadmap to unleash your potential and bring about long-lasting change, whether you're a leader, an aspiring influencer, or just someone who wants to have a positive impact.

Keep in mind that everyone has the potential to influence others; it is not just a power held by a small number of people. We can create a better world for ourselves and coming generations if we harness this ability and adopt the principles of How to Win Friends and Influence People.

Join me as we set off on this transforming trip.

Content

Introduction

Chapter 1: The Enigmatic Master

- Introduces the main character, a young person who is trying to understand the art of persuasion. Meeting with a strange tutor who is intelligent and has tremendous influence skills

-The protagonist is introduced to the idea of influence and its importance in all facets of life by the mentor. She also learns the basics of how perception and communication may be used to influence others.

Chapter 2: Exploring Your Internal Storyteller

- The mentor helps the protagonist identify their special narrative talents. Early attempts to use storytelling as a tool for influence and the lessons learnt along the way.

-Exploration of various storytelling strategies and their impact on influencing others. The protagonist learns to build engaging narratives that ring true with people's emotions and ideals.

Chapter 3: The Shades of Doubt

- The protagonist encounters both internal and external obstacles that put their faith in their capacity for influence to the test.

The mentor assists the protagonist in overcoming self-doubt and cultivating perseverance in the face of hardship. - Encounter with skeptics and critics who oppose the protagonist's pursuit of influence.

- A description of the significance of truthfulness and sincerity in the art of persuasion

Chapter 4: The Influential Quest

-Each encounter presents a different influencing challenge that the protagonist must overcome. The mentor offers advice and insight on how to adapt influence strategies to different situations.

- The protagonist develops their capacity for attentive listening, comprehending others' viewpoints, and adapting their approach appropriately.

Chapter 5 : The Ethical Dilemma

-The protagonist faces an ethical dilemma which puts their integrity and moral compass to the test. A mentor delivers lessons on the significance of ethical influence and the responsibility it entails.

-Dealing with the repercussions of unethical influence practices and the impact on relationships. The protagonist makes an important choice that determines their future as an ethical influencer.

Chapter 6: The Power of Teamwork

- The protagonist gains knowledge of the value of teamwork and collaboration in successful endeavors. Projects in which characters work together, each contributing their own special talents and viewpoints

- Resolving problems and locating common ground through skillful negotiation and communication. The protagonist learns about the multiplicative strength of group influence

Chapter 7: The Turning Point

point - It represents the apex of the protagonist's development into a powerful person. A turning point in the story when the protagonist's power reaches a critical mass and causes significant change

- A review of the development and transformation that have occurred throughout the narrative. Celebration of the influence made by the protagonist and the lessons they have learnt while learning the art of influencing

Chapter 8: The Lasting Impact of Influence

- The main character considers the legacy they want to leave as a powerful person. They inspire people to embrace the art of influence and make a positive difference in their own lives and communities by sharing their knowledge and talents with the next generation and by taking on the role of mentor themselves.

- F14inal thoughts on the influence's enduring impact and its possibilities for society and personal change

Chapter 9: The Psychology of Persuasion

- Exploration of the psychological principles and techniques that underlie effective influence

- Gaining an understanding of social proof, reciprocity, cognitive biases, and other persuasion tactics; - The protagonist learns how to use these psychological insights to ethically persuade others.

Chapter 10: Dealing with Obstacles and Resistance

- The protagonist comes across people that are resistive to their influence and learns how to get over opposition.

- An examination of typical stumbling blocks to persuasion and strategies for overcoming them - Overcoming self-doubt and setbacks and developing resilience in the face of difficulties

Chapter 11: Developing to Different Characters and Cultures

-The protagonist learns how to modify their approach to fit different personality types and cultural circumstances. Understanding the importance that personality types and cultural variances have in influencing others.

- Gaining knowledge on how to make meaningful connections by navigating cultural norms, values, and communication practices

Chapter 12: Influence in the Digital Era

-Understanding the dynamics of online communities, social media platforms, and virtual interactions, as well as utilizing digital tools and strategies for successful online influence and storytelling

Chapter 13: Influencing to Social Change

-The main character explores the world of social influence and advocacy for beneficial societal change. The protagonist learns how to use their influence to address social issues and have a significant impact

- Recognizing the value of grassroots movements, collective action, and public opinion.

Chapter 14: The Mastery of Non-Verbal Influence

-Understanding body language, facial expressions, and gestures can help you communicate with others effectively. explores the importance of non-verbal communication in influencing others.

- The main character gains the ability to recognize and use nonverbal signals for better rapport-building and influence.

Chapter 15: The Ever-Evolving Influence Journey

-Reflection on the protagonist's development and transformation throughout their influence journey is found

- Acknowledging that influence is a lifelong endeavor that requires constant learning and adaptation.

-Adopting the mindset of continuous improvement as an influential person.

Chapter 16: The Ripple Impact

-The protagonist observes how their influence has a cascading effect, encouraging others to take on similar roles.

- Examining how influence is interconnected and how one person's influence can cause a domino effect. Recognizing the group's ability to influence change for the better and forge a better future.

Influencing Minds is the game of your words

Chapter 1

The
Enigmatic Master

A young person by the name of Alex once lived in the thriving city of Viridian. Alex felt a lingering frustration with their inability to effectively influence others despite being talented and ambitious. Their ideas seemed to be ignored, and their efforts to persuade and motivate people frequently failed. Alex embarked on a search for the legendary mentor known for their extraordinary influence abilities because she was determined to learn the techniques of the art of influencing. Alex trudged through Viridian's maze-like streets in search of the mysterious mentor. Alex's heart was filled with hope as word spread throughout the city of the mentor's wisdom and insight. Finally, Alex found a modest cottage hidden in a beautiful garden in an isolated part of the city.

A figure with a partially-obscured face emerged from the shadows as they got closer to the cottage. The mentor they had been looking for was there. The mentor's piercing eyes appeared to be filled with a vast store of wisdom and experience. The mentor held out a hand, inviting Alex into their modest home without saying a word. The interior walls were covered with books and artifacts from distant lands, each one containing a tale of power and knowledge. The mentor indicated for Alex to sit down and then spoke in a gentle yet authoritative manner.

The mentor said, "Welcome, seeker of influence. "I've been waiting for you for a while. Influencing others is a delicate dance between the heart and the mind, not just a skill. You must first comprehend yourself and the intricacies of human nature in order to master influence. With that, the mentor began an engrossing account of their own development as an influence. They discussed their successes and setbacks, as well as the lessons they had learnt from their numerous interactions with people from various walks of life. Alex listened intently, absorbing up everything the mentor said like a sponge.

The mentor emphasized perception and communication throughout the dialogue as key elements in the art of persuading. They emphasized the importance of seeing past outward manifestations in order to comprehend the motivations behind people's behavior. The mentor emphasized the value of empathy and urged Alex to put himself in others' shoes in order to understand their viewpoint. The mentor wrapped up their story as the sun began to set and sent a lovely glow through the cottage windows. They looked intently at Alex while exchanging a knowing smile.

"The road to master the art of influencing now begins, my excited apprentice. We will work together to explore the depths of human connection, solve the riddles of persuasive communication, and help you realize your full potential. Alex realized that their fight for power had only just begun, which gave him newfound vigor. Knowing that Alex's perspective of influence would be shaped by their advice and that it would change their capacity to affect change in the world, they experienced a wave of thankfulness for having found the mentor. Alex stepped out into the darkness as they said goodbye to the mentor's cottage, eager to see what was ahead and with a renewed feeling of purpose. Alex was prepared to start their transformative journey, determined to master the art of persuasion, armed with the mentor's advice and ready to face the obstacles and revelations that lay ahead. Little did they realize that the true meaning of influence would go well beyond their own goals, affecting the lives of countless others and determining Viridian's future.

Chapter 2
Exploring Your Internal Storyteller

After their meeting with the mentor, Alex's mind was constantly thinking ahead and asking questions. They couldn't help but wonder what lay in store for them as they set out to become experts in persuasion. Alex returned to their regular life eager to learn more about the mentor's lessons and with a strong drive to realize their full influence potential.

One idea reverberated in Alex's mind as they considered the mentor's advice: the potency of storytelling. They came to see that stories had a special power to enthrall, motivate, and move people. Stories had the capacity to go beyond logical justifications and reach the very essence of human feeling.

Alex set out on a journey of self-discovery with the goal of releasing their inner storyteller. They looked for stories from various civilizations and researched the history of storytelling. They consumed a lot of books and films, and they even looked out regional storytellers who would impart their knowledge at events and festivals.

One night, under a blanket of stars, Alex happened across a little community renowned for its longstanding storytelling tradition. The villagers exchanged myths and traditions that had been passed down through the ages as they congregated around a roaring fire. Their eyes sparkled with the warmth of the fire, and the listeners' minds were filled with vivid images thanks to the melodious rhythm of their voices.

They saw patterns emerge as Alex took in the stories. The tales that touched on themes like love, sorrow, overcoming adversity, and the strength of hope resonated with people the most. These narratives sparked feelings of empathy and long-lasting impressions.

Alex started writing their own stories after being inspired by the villagers' storytellers. They mastered the art of weaving words together to evoke various emotions and vivid visuals. They experimented with various narrative devices like suspense, humor, and metaphor after realizing that each had a different effect on the audience.

The ever-observant tutor saw Alex's developing narrative talent. They created an atmosphere where they could hone their abilities and get priceless feedback by inviting Alex to share their stories. With each storytelling session, Alex developed their confidence and improved their capacity to captivate an audience, engage them, and make a lasting impression.

Alex found a way to connect people's individual experiences and worldviews with one another through storytelling. They understood that true stories, taken from their own experiences, had the capacity to evoke strong emotions and spur action. They knew that they could create real connections with others and shape their viewpoints by being open and honest about their struggles, victories, and lessons learned.

Alex came to the realization that storytelling was more than just engaging or amusing an audience as they travelled further. It was a tool that could be used with aim and purpose. It served as a vehicle for expressing values, supporting change, and motivating people to take action.

With the help of the mentor's lessons and the skill of storytelling, Alex set out on a journey to have a positive impact on their town. They began by discussing their own instances of fortitude in order to demonstrate the transforming potential of tenacity. People listened, their hearts moved by Alex's tales' realism and reliability.

They soon found themselves at the centre of debates and collaborations aimed at addressing societal concerns as word of Alex's impact spread. Their experiences acted as catalysts, starting discussions, encouraging empathy, and motivating group action.

Alex felt more assured in their capacity for impact as time went on. They observed the effect their stories had on people, how it opened up fresh viewpoints and created a desire for change. The once-disgruntled person had transformed into a skilled influencer, spinning narratives that permanently etched themselves into hearts and minds.

Alex realized that narrating stories was just the beginning as Chapter 2 came to a close. They had only begun to explore the art of persuasion, and they still had a world of opportunities ahead of them. With their newly acquired narrative talent, Alex eagerly sought the mentor's advice on the following stage of their influencing journey in order to explore the more intricate facets of the practice and have an even bigger impact.

Chapter 3
The Shades of Doubt

Alex came to the realization that storytelling was only one aspect of the intricate web of influence as they travelled further with the mentor. They realized that in order to properly master the art of influencing, they had to develop strong relationships with other people and earn their trust. The mentor led Alex to their next lesson, which was on the skill of forming bridges, after realizing the value of trust in influence.

Alex was taken by the mentor to a busy market in a nearby town. The trainer pointed out a seller known for their outstanding repute amongst the commotion of consumers and dealers. The vendor effortlessly connected with their clients by greeting them with a warm smile and a genuine smile, which helped to create trust.

By observing how the vendor interacted with customers, Alex picked some important trust-building tips. They found that the foundation for building strong friendships was real empathy and attentive listening. The supplier shown genuine interest in the client's lives by taking the time to comprehend their needs, wants, and worries.

The coach urged Alex to put these abilities to use by conversing with customers. They addressed people with curiosity and an interest in

learning about their viewpoints and past experiences. Alex observed that
when they conversed, a deeper level of trust developed when they paid
attention to others' perspectives and demonstrated empathy.

Trust, according to the mentor, was like a weak bridge that bound
two people together. To understand and support each other, it took
fostering, care, and a sincere goal. As people were more likely to be
sensitive to ideas and opinions when they had a true connection, Alex
realized that developing trust was a critical first step in influencing
others.

Alex engaged themselves in the skill of creating trusting relationships
in the days that followed. They looked for chances to interact with a
variety of people from various spheres of life and backgrounds. They
engaged in active listening, posed probing questions, and showed
genuine empathy.

They learned the value of authenticity as Alex created trusting bridges between them. They came to the conclusion that in order to properly connect with others, they had to value their own distinctive perspectives and life experiences. They let others see their true selves by sharing personal experiences, flaws, and victories. Others started to open up in response, fostering a climate of understanding and cooperation.

Through their conversations, Alex also discovered the value of honesty and reliability in establishing trust. They were aware that their words and deeds needed to match and that lack of consistency or follow-through could quickly undermine trust. Alex increased the confidence they had gained from others by keeping their word and proving their dependability.

The mentor urged Alex to consider the bridges they had made as they proceeded to lead them on their influential journey. Alex realized the beneficial effects they were having on people and their neighborhood. They were more effective at influencing people because they concentrated on developing trust and true connections.

Alex was excited to investigate the next aspect of the art of influencing as Chapter 3 drew to an end. They felt empowered to develop even deeper relationships and motivate change in the lives of those around them because they had a greater appreciation for trust-building and the bridges they had built. Their guru, who served as their continuous guide, was ready to help them negotiate the next stage of their important endeavor.

Chapter 4
The Influential Quest

Alex's adventure led them to explore the field of emotional intelligence as part of their ongoing quest to master the art of persuading. The mentor understood the importance of emotional intelligence as a tool for truly comprehending and connecting with others. The mentor then started teaching Alex about the power of emotions after coming to this realization.

The mentor and Alex set out to attend a nearby theatre, which was renowned for its stirring performances that moved its audience. Alex was drawn into a world of unfiltered emotions and engrossing storytelling as they sat under the theater's dim lighting. Everyone in attendance was affected by the performances, which generated emotions such as happiness, despair, rage, and empathy.

The mentor and Alex had a conversation on how emotions affect other people after the show. They looked at the significance of emotional awareness—both of one's own feelings and those of others. The mentor emphasized the importance of understanding people' emotions because doing so opens the door to developing sincere relationships and comprehending their viewpoints.

Alex's emotional intelligence was being developed, therefore the mentor introduced them to numerous activities and methods. In order to better grasp how different emotions affected their thoughts and behaviors, they practiced identifying and labeling their own emotions. In order to properly manage their emotions and navigate interpersonal relationships, they needed to be self-aware.

The mentor then exhorted Alex to develop empathy by actively listening and making an effort to comprehend the feelings that underlie other people's words and behaviors. Alex was able to assume various emotional states through role-playing activities, which helped them refine their capacity to react sensitively and compassionately.

Alex started to pick up on subtle hints and non-verbal expressions that expressed emotions as their emotional intelligence increased. They developed the ability to read body language, facial expressions, and vocal tones, which improved their capacity for deeper interpersonal connections. Alex realized that in order to persuade people, he needed to appeal to both their emotions and their intellect.

The idea of emotional contagion—the idea that feelings can spread from one person to another—was also discussed by the mentor and Alex. They talked on the value of developing happy feelings within oneself because it affected those around them. Alex had the ability to inspire others and foster an environment that was favorable to influence by exuding positivism and optimism.

The mentor constantly emphasized to Alex during their training that emotional intelligence should be combined with honesty and a sincere desire to help others. The goal was to comprehend and relate to others in a meaningful and moral way, not to manipulate emotions for one's own benefit.

As Chapter 4 came to an end, Alex had gained a greater understanding of emotional intelligence. They were aware of the influence that emotions can have and how empathy, self-awareness, and genuine concern serve as the cornerstones of lasting relationships. With this newfound knowledge, Alex was prepared to further their comprehension and continue developing their abilities in the art of influencing. He excitedly anticipated the mentor's advice on the next chapter of their influential journey.

Chapter 5
The Ethical Dilemma

The mentor realized the importance of persuasive communication as Alex proceeded to learn the skill of persuading. They realized that the secret to expressing ideas, motivating others to act, and influencing others was effective communication. In light of this, the mentor started instructing Alex in the craft of persuasion.

The mentor led Alex to a busy marketplace where sellers jostled for consumers and attention. They saw how certain sellers had no trouble grabbing people's attention while other vendors had trouble standing out. Clarity, conviction, and empathy were highlighted as important components of compelling communication by the mentor.

Alex was once more introduced to the power of storytelling by their mentor in order to aid them in honing their persuasive communication abilities. They pushed Alex to craft stories that captured the listener's attention, stirred feelings, and produced an unforgettable experience.

Alex was able to present their thoughts in an engaging and approachable way through narrative.

The mentor then concentrated on the skill of good listening. They emphasized that effective persuasive communication required not only talking but also truly comprehending the needs and viewpoints of others. Alex discovered the value of probing inquiries, attentive listening, and message customization to appeal to the particular issues and aspirations of their audience.

The mentor also helped Alex grasp the significance of nonverbal cues. They looked at the role that body language, vocal tonality, and facial expressions have in expressing assurance, veracity, and authenticity. Alex trained adopting an open, self-assured stance, keeping eye contact, and modulating their voice to match the nuanced emotional content of their communication.

The mentor taught Alex about developing a logical argument as they studied persuasive communication in greater depth. They showed them how to compile information, conduct data analysis, and offer strong arguments in favor of their positions. Alex developed the ability to foresee objections and respond to them logically, enabling their audience to recognize the necessity and worth of their suggestions.

However, the mentor emphasized to Alex that effective communication required an emotional appeal as well and that it was not just about reasoning. Alex learned how to link his arguments to the fundamental principles and ambitions of his audience. Alex might create a stronger connection and spur action by exhibiting empathy and illustrating how their suggestions could benefit others.

In role-playing activities, the mentor and Alex practiced persuasive communication throughout their course by simulating numerous circumstances. With the knowledge that effective influence meant adjusting their messages to the particular needs, interests, and beliefs of their listeners, Alex learned to change their communication approach to various audiences.

Alex had learned more about persuasive communication as Chapter 5 came to a close. They had mastered the art of inspiring and involving others through active listening, storytelling, logical argument, and emotional appeal. With these resources at their disposal, Alex felt more assured in their capacity to persuade others to change for the better.

While praising Alex's development, the mentor also emphasized the need for ongoing practice and improvement if one was to truly master the art of influencing. So, ready to study more aspects of the influential journey and reach their full potential in the art of influencing, Alex excitedly anticipated the mentor's advice for the next chapter.

Chapter 6
The Power of Teamwork

The problem of opposition from others arose as Alex advanced on their path to mastering the art of influencing. The mentor led Alex down a path of comprehension and cooperation because they understood that overcoming resistance requires a careful balance of empathy and teamwork.

The mentor arranged for Alex to take part in a group project where various team members had divergent opinions in order to probe deeper into this subject. The mentor clarified that this activity would provide Alex a chance to practice empathic listening and group problem-solving.

Alex met opposition from team members who had strong opinions about their own ideas over the course of the project. Alex took a calm and sympathetic stance rather than getting into a fight. They took the time to hear each team member's issues and points of view in order to better grasp their driving forces.

The mentor emphasized the value of having empathy when trying to persuade others. They claimed that Alex could understand the anxieties, insecurities, or prior experiences that influenced the opinions of those who were opposed to their beliefs by placing himself in their position. With this knowledge, Alex was able to address their issues and create a common ground.

In order to overcome resistance, teamwork became a crucial tactic. The mentor gave Alex advice on how to lead inclusive and open sessions in which team members were urged to voice their opinions and actively participate in problem-solving. Alex promoted a culture of shared ownership and involvement in the project's success through group brainstorming and consensus-building exercises.

The mentor gave examples of influential people who had overcome opposition by working together and showing empathy. They talked about how these people could relate to others more deeply, understanding their problems, and coming up with cooperative solutions. Alex absorbed these lessons and found inspiration in the powerful figures who had set the route in front of them.

Alex refined their abilities in teamwork, conflict resolution, and empathic listening during their training. They used active listening skills, paraphrased other people's viewpoints to ensure understanding, and looked for solutions that would benefit everyone. Through these drills, Alex gained the capacity to handle resistance with collaboration and grace.

As Chapter 6 came to a close, Alex had learned important lessons about getting over opposition through teamwork and empathy. They realized that persuading people frequently involved confronting opposition head-on with understanding and a willingness to cooperate in order to achieve a shared objective. Alex anxiously anticipated the mentor's advice for the following chapter as they were prepared to continue their influential journey with compassion and a collaborative spirit and their improved empathy and teamwork skills.

Chapter 7
The Turning Point

Alex had spent a lot of time advocating for better education in Peritonea, attending endless meetings, and conducting exhaustive research. Years had been spent cultivating connections with important players, mobilizing the community, and raising public awareness of the urgent need for educational reform. Alex couldn't help but feel as though they were at a turning point that may advance their efforts and usher in the revolutionary change they had been working towards. As they continued to put their all into the cause, this sensation grew stronger.

One day, while Alex was getting ready for yet another neighborhood gathering, they got an unexpected call. It was Maya, a vivacious and passionate person who had just finished attending a town hall on education. Maya stated her sincere desire to work with Alex in order to increase their influence and offered her love for his work.

Maya's enthusiasm and resolve intrigued Alex, who agreed to meet for coffee. They identified a shared vision for school reform during their conversation, which complemented one another's opinions and strong points. They understood that working together may potentially lead to a tipping point—a time when their combined efforts could spark a wave of transformation in Peritonea's educational system.

Wanting to make the most of their newly formed alliance, Alex and Maya came up with creative ideas for ways to involve the neighborhood and win over support for their cause. They made the decision to plan a number of community forums, seminars, and panel discussions where people from all backgrounds could come together to talk about the urgent problems and potential answers related to education reform. The activities immediately acquired pace, attracting notable individuals from the education sector and the attention of local media sources. People started to notice the enthusiasm, knowledge, and sincere concern that both Maya and Alex exuded. As the news got out, interest and involvement in the community soared, reaching a breaking point where the need for change became too strong to ignore.

Alex and Maya successfully pushed the Veritonian school board for a meeting thanks to their combined power. They presented their case with conviction and supported it with data-driven research, personal experiences, and the resounding backing of the community. They had a complete solution that addressed the systemic difficulties faced by poor children. The unanimous support from the public and Alex & Maya's specific   recommendations   moved   the   board

members. They agreed to work together and put the suggested changes in the educational system of Veritonia into effect after realizing the potential for dramatic change.

The announcement of the board's decision travelled quickly, adding to the community's enthusiasm and sense of accomplishment. It was clear that Alex and Maya's efforts had finally reached a turning point, which signaled the start of a new age in Peritonea.

Alex and Maya realized their work was far from done after the reforms were put into motion. They were aware that continuing cooperation, lobbying, and unwavering commitment were necessary to maintain the momentum and ensure the successful implementation of the reforms. It was up to them to direct the strong change momentum that had been sparked by the tipping point in the proper directions.

Alex and Maya kept up their tireless work in the months and years that followed, cultivating alliances, keeping track of development, and encouraging others to take charge of the cause. Their influence extended beyond Peritonea, motivating people and groups in close-by cities and even other parts of the nation to support educational change in their own areas.

As Alex and Maya thought back on the path that had brought them to the turning point, they understood that it was the result of not just their own efforts but the combined strength of an entire community brought together by a common goal. Collectively, they had demonstrated how influence, when used wisely, has the power to reshape lives and entire societies.

Alex and Maya looked ahead to the difficulties that lied beyond the tipping point with hearts full of appreciation and a renewed sense of purpose. They realized that maintaining change required alertness, flexibility, and constant dedication. They were aware that their influence would be vital in directing Veritonia's educational system towards excellence and equity in the future.

The tipping point has awoken the community as well. Coming forward with a desire to add their voices and efforts to the ongoing reform process were parents, educators, and students. Together, they created a group of ardent supporters and collaborated with Alex and Maya to make sure that each and every child in Peritonea had access to a high-quality education.

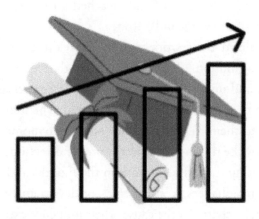

The effects of the tipping point became clear as the years went by. Graduation rates increased, student performance improved, and formerly underserved communities had more access to higher education. The educational system in Peritonea rose to prominence as a brilliant illustration of the transformative potential of group influence and dedication to change.

Beyond Peritonea, word of the tipping point's success was widely disseminated. Alex and Maya received invitations to speak at conferences, offer their perspectives to decision-makers, and provide consultation on school reform initiatives in other towns and cities. Their influence spread beyond their immediate neighborhood, encouraging countless others to trust in the efficacy of group effort and the possibility of positive change.

In the end, the turning point was more than simply a split second; it served as the impetus for a sustained movement. It served as a reminder to Alex, Maya, and the entire community of the amazing things that may be accomplished when people work together for a common goal. It reaffirmed the idea that influence, when used sensibly and passionately, has the power to overcome obstacles, alter systems, and usher in a better future for everybody.

Alex and Maya realized that the tipping point was only the beginning as they reflected on their trip. They were aware that their work would go on, developing and adapting to the shifting demands and difficulties of the educational environment in Veritonia. Together, they would work through the difficulties, rely on their shared purpose for support, and build on the momentum started at the tipping point.

We may all learn from the tale of the tipping point that influence can bring about significant change if it is used with purpose, empathy, and persistence. It exhorts us to seize the chance to create tipping moments on our own, to have faith in our ability to change things, and to work together with others to build a better future.

The journey of Alex and Maya continues as the chapter on the turning point comes to an end. Their influence, sparked by the tipping point, serves as a source of inspiration and hope for future generations. They move forward hand in hand, firm in their conviction that collective influence can create a world where every kid has the chance to flourish and reach their full potential.

Chapter 8
The Lasting Impact of Influence

The mentor explained the idea of leaving a lasting legacy as Alex's significant journey came to an end. They emphasized the fact that real influence might affect the future and went beyond the present. The mentor provided tales of significant individuals who had made a significant impact on the world to go deeper into this subject. They talked about how these people had utilized their power to affect change for the better, leaving a lasting legacy that would inspire and affect future generations. Alex understood that having a clear purpose was necessary for leaving a lasting impact. The mentor prompted them to consider their core beliefs, areas of interest, and the contribution they desired to contribute to the world. Alex could leave a lasting impression on people by conducting their affairs in a manner consistent with their ideals and concentrating on a worthwhile goal.

The exercises the mentor led Alex through clarified their vision for their legacy. They looked into many ways they could leave a lasting impression, whether it be through their work, involvement in the community, or lobbying for a subject that was important to them. Alex started to realize how crucial it was to discover one's individual voice and use it to effect change.

The mentor emphasized the value of honesty and integrity throughout their training in order to leave a lasting legacy. They talked about how powerful people were renowned for their unwavering adherence to their principles and their capacity to motivate others through their deeds. Alex discovered that people may leave a lasting legacy if they remained true to their values and principles.

In order to empower others to become influential in their own right, Alex was urged by his mentor to look beyond his or her own accomplishments. They talked about how crucial it is to mentor and assist upcoming leaders while also transferring information and experience to the following generation. Alex understood that by supporting others, they may increase their impact for a very long time. Alex developed their own idea for their enduring legacy as Chapter 8 went on. They understood that making a difference in the world requires a mix of intention, doing, and motivating others to continue the cause. Alex was excited and overwhelmed with responsibility as they considered the legacy they would leave behind.

The mentor emphasized to Alex that creating a lasting legacy required a lifetime of dedication. They exhorted them to stay committed to their goals, to keep honing their vision, and to adjust it to the ever-changing demands of the outside world. By accomplishing this, Alex would leave behind a lasting legacy that would have an impact on people's lives for all time.

Alex experienced a strong sense of purpose and the desire to leave a lasting legacy as Chapter 8 came to a close. They were aware that they could change the future for the better and that their influence would last well beyond their own lifetimes. Alex was ready to embrace their role as a visionary leader and leave a lasting legacy of good change as they excitedly anticipated the mentor's advice for the final stages of their influential journey. With their vision clear and their resolve steadfast, Alex awaited the mentor's instruction with anticipation.

Chapter 9
The Psychology of Persuasion

Alex had always been supportive of using persuasion as a technique to bring about change. They realized that effective persuasion required more than just persuading others to share their point of view; it also required understanding the psychology of decision-making and adapting their strategy accordingly. They came to the realization that persuasion was a complicated interaction of numerous psychological aspects as Alex dug deeper into the study of it. They discovered that by utilizing these characteristics, they could improve their persuasiveness and raise the possibility that they would succeed in accomplishing their goals.

The idea of reciprocity was the first thing Alex looked at. They realized that when someone did them a favor or helped them out, people naturally wanted to return the favor. Using this information, Alex concentrated on establishing sincere relationships with people and figuring out methods to be of use to them before making any demands. They built a base of trust and reciprocity by acting with goodwill and generosity, which set the platform for persuasiveness.

Alex continued by exploring the psychology of social proof. They understood that people frequently observe the thoughts, feelings, and behaviors of others for guidance. Knowing this, Alex cleverly used social proof by presenting endorsements, success tales, and proof that others had previously taken up their cause. They furthered the impression that their cause was both well-liked and worthwhile by highlighting the rising number of people joining their campaign.

Alex then introduced the idea of scarcity to them. They understood that products that were rare or had restricted availability tended to be valued more highly by people. By using this theory, they developed their persuasive arguments to emphasize the rare and constrained chances for people to participate. Alex inspired others to act right away out of a sense of urgency and exclusivity since they could miss out otherwise.

Alex also looked at the concept of authority as a psychological factor. They knew that requests from people they regarded as informed and credible were more likely to be complied with. Alex put time and effort into developing their expertise, remaining current with new findings and advancements in their industry, and making connections with other respected experts and influencers in order to establish their authority. By presenting themselves as a reliable source of knowledge and direction, they won the audience's respect and trust, which increased the potency of their persuasive strategies. And finally, Alex understood the importance of emotions in persuasion. They recognized that people first made emotional decisions before rationalizing them. With the help of this knowledge, Alex carefully structured their communications to arouse strong feelings while appealing to the fears, hopes, and aspirations of their audience. Alex was able to make their argument more personal and captivating by appealing to their emotions and connecting with them on a deeper level.

With this knowledge of persuasion psychology at his disposal, Alex tackled their advocacy activities with fresh insight and dexterity. They adjusted their speeches, interactions, and messages to reflect the concepts they had learnt. They gradually saw a notable improvement in their capacity to persuade others and win people over to their cause.

On the other hand, as Alex travelled further, they were aware of the moral obligation that comes with persuasive influence. They understood the significance of employing their abilities in an ethical and responsible manner, making sure that their persuasive actions were motivated by a sincere concern for other people's welfare and the larger good.

Alex considered the influence of persuasion and its potential for good as Chapter 9 came to a close. They realized that they could effectively convey their message, rally support, and elicit action by utilizing the psychology of persuasion. They vowed to utilize their influencing skills to shape the world in which their cause might flourish and leave a lasting impression as they accepted their duty as a powerful advocate. Alex eagerly anticipated the chapters that lay ahead, eager to continue their persuasive journey and make a difference in the lives of others. With a thorough understanding of the psychology of persuasion and a solid dedication to ethical influence, Alex looked forward to them. They were aware that the psychology of persuasion would continue to form the basis of their advocacy work, but they also understood the necessity of constant improvement.

Alex reinforced their dedication to perfecting their abilities, remaining aware of the changing requirements and preferences of their audience, and consistently modifying their approach as they finished the chapter on the psychology of persuasion. They were aware that persuasive communication requires a careful balancing act between strategy, empathy, and authenticity.

Alex became aware of the value of teamwork and the strength of group influence. They realized that by collaborating with other like-minded specialists and activists, they could strengthen their argument and develop a message that was more unified and persuasive. They actively sought out chances to work together, exchange information, and pick the brains of people who had perfected the art of persuasion in their own special ways.

Alex looked forward to discovering more aspects of influence and expanding their knowledge of the art of persuasion in the chapters to come. They were aware that persuasion was a dynamic and complex talent, and they were eager to learn new perceptions and methods to strengthen their capacity for influence.

They experienced a sense of hope and excitement as Alex concluded Chapter 9. They had a stronger grasp of the psychology of persuasion and a reaffirmed dedication to ethical influence. They understood the power of persuasion to influence people's thoughts, alter their behavior, and leave a lasting impression when employed sensibly and with the greater good in mind. With this fresh insight and determination, Alex eagerly anticipated the difficulties and chances that were ahead. They were eager to continue their influential journey and have a significant impact on the globe, and they were prepared to embrace the following chapters.

The chapters that would follow would deepen their understanding of influence and offer doors to new opportunities, Alex realized as she flipped the pages. They were dedicated to using persuasion's power while always being aware of its potential and the responsibilities that went along with it.

With each new chapter, Alex's influence became greater and their commitment to enacting change became more intense. They were equipped with empathy, honesty, and a steadfast dedication to their cause and were motivated to successfully negotiate the difficulties of influence.

Alex experienced a fresh feeling of purpose and drive as they excitedly flipped the page to Chapter 10. They were prepared to take on the challenges and opportunities that were ahead as they continued to write one chapter at a time, knowing that their adventure had only just begun.

Chapter 10
Dealing With Obstacles And Resistance

The capacity to negotiate opposition and overcome hurdles was a critical lesson the mentor taught Alex as they progressed on their path to mastering the art of influencing. The mentor was aware that not everyone would readily accept new concepts or viewpoints and that influencing others often presented difficulties. The mentor accompanied Alex to a town hall meeting where a contentious discussion was taking place to demonstrate this point. Diverse groups held opposite viewpoints and vehemently upheld them. Alex watched as people's feelings were intense and they got firmly rooted in their own views.

The mentor clarified that when attempting to influence others, resistance and challenges are unavoidable. They stressed the significance of handling these difficulties with tolerance, understanding, and an open mind. The mentor gave Alex advice on how to deal with resistance and turn setbacks into chances for improvement.

First, the mentor showed Alex the value of active listening despite conflict. They advised Alex to try to comprehend the worries, apprehensions, and underlying motives of individuals who opposed their beliefs. Alex might encourage an atmosphere of respect and free speech by paying close attention while listening and taking into account the opinions of others. The mentor then taught Alex the skill of coming to an understanding. They indicated that Alex may overcome divergent opinions by identifying similar ideals, objectives, or aspirations. They put into practice strategies like reframing the discussion, emphasizing common goals, and looking for win-win solutions that addressed the issues on both sides.

The mentor also taught Alex how to control their own feelings when they encounter opposition. Even in the midst of contentious debates, they learned how to maintain their composure and demonstrate empathy. Alex might affect the conversation's tone and preserve a positive mood by keeping grounded and reacting with grace and understanding. The mentor discussed historical examples of notable people who overcame great challenges in their quest for change as they and the group dug deeper into the subject of negotiating opposition. They emphasized the tenacity, fortitude, and steadfast faith in their cause that allowed these individuals to persevere in the face of difficulty and ultimately impact others.

Alex discovered that obstacles and failures were a necessary component on the road to influence. The mentor emphasized the value

of fortitude and gaining knowledge from these situations. They urged Alex to see challenges as chances for development and to regard each failure as a chance to improve their strategy and deepen their conviction. Throughout their training, Alex applied these techniques in a variety of situations. They practiced negotiating conversations with empathy, patience, and resilience through role-playing activities where they confronted recalcitrant people. Over time, Alex noticed how they could create understanding with people who at first appeared to be resistant to change.

As Chapter 10 came to a close, Alex had acquired a useful set of abilities and viewpoints for navigating opposition and overcoming challenges. They realized that influencing others frequently demanded tenacity, suppleness, and a sincere desire to comprehend other viewpoints. Alex excitedly awaited the mentor's advice for the following chapter, ready to continue their influential adventure with resiliency and determination. With newfound confidence and a deeper grasp of the art of negotiating opposition, Alex awaited the mentor's instruction with anticipation.

Chapter 11
Developing to Different Characters and Cultures

They came into a wide variety of people with various personalities, racial backgrounds, and cultural viewpoints as Alex's influence grew. They understood that in order to effectively connect and influence people, they needed to learn how to modify their strategy in light of these variations. Alex recognized that every person they came into contact with had a unique set of values, beliefs, and communication methods. They understood that what spoke to one individual might not speak to another in the same way. They therefore needed to be flexible and sensitive to these distinctions in order to forge meaningful relationships and exert influence over others.

Alex's initial step was to hone his powers of active listening and sharp observation. They observed both verbal and nonverbal cues, noting people's communication preferences, styles, and cultural quirks. Alex learned important lessons about how to approach and connect with each person they encountered by watching and listening. Alex was also aware of the value of empathy in comprehending various cultures and personalities. They deliberately tried to place themselves in other people's situations and saw the world from their point of view. They were able to have a genuine awareness for the diverse experiences and principles that influenced everyone's behavior and ideas as a result of this.

Using this knowledge, Alex modified their communication style to suit the needs of the people they were interacting with. They changed their vocabulary, tone, and tempo to establish a friendly and relatable atmosphere for deep conversation. They understood that in order to effectively influence others, one must meet them where they were rather than imposing their own communication style on them.

Alex also wanted to promote inclusivity and cross cultural divides. They invested the time to learn about the values, traditions, and cultural sensitivities of the various populations they interacted with. They were able to do this to avoid inadvertent misunderstandings or disputes as they navigated cultural differences with respect and understanding. Alex recognized the value of using storytelling to bridge cultural divides. They understood the power of storytelling to bridge cultural divides and forge meaningful emotional relationships. Alex was able to connect with people from different backgrounds by including personal stories and experiences into their communications.

They observed how their efforts had a good effect as Alex persisted in tailoring their strategy to various personalities and cultural contexts. They built rapport and genuine ties with those who may have been initially hesitant or skeptic. Alex gained the trust and respect of people from all walks of life by exhibiting cultural awareness and adaptability. Alex understood the need for constant learning and humility when it came to adjusting to various personalities and cultures. They recognized that acquiring cultural competency was a lifelong process and that they would invariably face fresh problems and challenges that called for more development and comprehension.

Alex considered the important lessons he had learnt about adjusting to other personalities and cultures as Chapter 11 came to a close. They came to see that effective influence required more than just the dissemination of knowledge; it also required the capacity to relate to people on a personal level and recognize and value their individual points of view. Alex anticipated the chapters that were ahead with a fresh dedication to cultural awareness and flexibility. They were eager to deepen their grasp of the rich diversity of the world around them because they were aware that the path of impact would continue to bring possibilities for learning and progress.

Alex carried the priceless knowledge gained about the potential of the digital era with them as they turned the page to Chapter 12. They were prepared to meet new people, accept new obstacles, and carry on their influential journey with empathy, respect, and a steadfast dedication to bridging cultural and racial divides.

Chapter 12
Influence of Digital Era

As Alex's path to influence grew, they discovered themselves in a more and more digital world where networking, information sharing, and communication could be done at the touch of a button. They understood the need to modify their influence tactics to fit the realities of the digital age, utilizing technology to magnify their message and reach a larger audience.

Alex recognized that the era of digital technology offered both opportunities and difficulties for impact. On the one hand, it provided a sizable platform for connecting with people beyond regional borders, facilitating the quick transmission of knowledge and concepts. On the other side, it presented difficulties including information overload, digital diversions, and the requirement to efficiently use new communication channels.

Alex entered the realm of social media, embracing the promise of the digital age and realizing its potential as a vehicle for impact. They developed a strong online presence by utilizing websites like Twitter, Integra, and LinkedIn to share insightful information, have important discussions, and build a community of like-minded people. Alex was also aware of the value of narrative in the digital age. They understood that gripping stories might capture internet audiences and motivate action. In light of this, they created engrossing and genuine tales that connected with their fans, grabbing their attention in the midst of the digital din, and encouraging a sense of community and shared purpose.

Alex also understood the value of visual content in the digital era. They utilized the effectiveness of pictures, films, and info graphics to present their ideas in a comprehensible and aesthetically pleasing manner. They were able to clearly explain complicated ideas and captivate their audience on various sensory levels by utilizing the visual medium. Alex followed the newest trends and technology as the digital world changed. They investigated cutting-edge methods and platforms that provided fresh opportunities for influence, including podcasts, live streaming, and virtual reality. They made sure that their influence remained applicable and powerful by adjusting to the rapidly shifting digital context.

However, Alex was also aware of how crucial it was in the digital age to maintain authenticity. They understood that developing trust and credibility with their online audience required being open, sincere, and consistent in their participation. They valued every opportunity to communicate and exert influence, giving replying to messages and comments top priority. Alex had to navigate the digital age while being aware of its dangers. They were aware of the risks associated with false information and the requirement to carefully consider online sources. They exhorted their adherents to exercise critical thought and to research material before accepting it as true.

Alex considered how the digital era's revolutionary force had shaped their ascent to prominence as Chapter 12 came to a close. They realized that embracing the internet world has increased their reach, allowing them to affect people they might not have otherwise come into contact with. Alex eagerly anticipated the chapters that were ahead, with a strong respect for the opportunities and responsibilities that the digital era brought. They were determined to remaining at the forefront of digital influence and utilizing technology to bring about significant change because they were aware that the digital landscape would continue to change.

Turning to Chapter 13, Alex brought with them a digital toolset of tactics, a dedication to authenticity, and a determination to maximize the power of the digital age. In the dynamic realm of digital communication, they were prepared to innovate, adapt, and continue on their impact path.

Chapter 13
Influencing to Social Change

The mentor stressed the value of tailoring Alex's communication approach to various people and circumstances as they continued their quest to perfect the art of persuasion. They understood that the capacity to connect with a range of personalities was necessary for effective influence, and they adjusted their strategy appropriately. The mentor and Alex went to a networking event to discuss this subject, where they spoke with plenty of people from different walks of life. They studied how various people interacted with one another, noting their preferences, communication techniques, and non-verbal cues.

The mentor clarified that understanding the particular requirements, preferences, and values of others was necessary in order to adapt to various communication styles. They emphasized the significance of adapting and being adaptable in order to forge deep ties and promote efficient communication. Alex discovered that some people enjoyed clear, concise communication while others valued more thorough justifications and first-person stories. In order to discern the communication style of the individual they were conversing with, the mentor advised them to carefully observe and listen.

They worked on mimicking the vocabulary, tone, and pace used by others in conversation. Alex could develop a connection with and foster a sense of understanding with their audience by matching their communication style to that of their listeners.

The mentor also emphasized the value of nonverbal cues in adjusting to various communication styles. They talked on how crucial it is to pay attention to others' body language, facial expressions, and gestures in order to understand their feelings and preferences. Alex discovered how to modify his or her own nonverbal clues to fit and create a more harmonic connection. The mentor gave examples of well-known people who had a remarkable ability to connect with various audiences as they discussed the subject of adjusting to various communication styles. They talked about how these people were able to motivate and sway others by being aware of and accommodating their particular communication preferences.

The mentor pushed Alex to develop empathy and active listening skills so that she could better comprehend the needs and viewpoints of many people. Alex had to negotiate talks with persons who had different communication styles throughout their role-playing

activities. Through these activities, Alex improved their capacity for flexibility, encouraging efficient communication and developing a rapport with a wide spectrum of people. During their training, Alex improved their sensitivity to the minute differences in communication styles. They developed the ability to identify the verbal and nonverbal clues that others used to communicate their preferences, changing their own speech in order to forge closer connections.

As Chapter 13 came to a close, Alex had gained a deeper understanding of the significance of customizing their communication approach to various people and circumstances. They realized that being able to connect truly and deeply with a range of personalities was necessary for effective influence. Alex excitedly anticipated the mentor's advice for the next chapter as they prepared to continue their impactful adventure with adaptability and the ability to interact with a wider spectrum of people. They had learned how to adapt to various communication methods.

Chapter 14
The Mastery of Non-Verbal Influence

Alex understood the value of nonverbal cues in building rapport, influencing views, and effectively communicating along their influence journey. They realized that becoming a more effective and compelling communicator required understanding non-verbal influence. Alex studied non-verbal communication in depth, looking at the numerous components that had a big impact on how people interacted with each other. They learned that subtle yet strong messages could be sent through body language, facial expressions, gestures, and even tone of voice, which may either support or undermine their efforts to persuade.

Alex paid particular attention to body language. They were aware of the potential for their posture, stance, and general body language to communicate assurance, openness, and credibility. They worked on projecting confidence, maintaining eye contact, and utilizing deliberate motions to captivate their audience and emphasize their point. Alex also observed their facial expressions intently, understanding how a sincere grin, alert facial clues, and a kind demeanor might forge an immediate connection with others. They mastered the art of using their facial expressions to portray warmth, empathy, and passion in order to make their audience feel at ease and open to their influence.

Alex was aware of the significance of vocal signals in non-verbal communication in addition to body language and facial emotions. To adapt their speech to the emotional context of their message, they practiced changing their tone, pitch, and rate of speech. They could arouse emotions, emphasize important topics, and draw the audience's attention by skillfully modulating their voice. Alex enhanced their active listening abilities to further their command of non-verbal influence. They understood that communicating their own messages was crucial, but so was actually listening to others—paying them full attention, nodding, and giving encouraging cues. Alex was able to influence others more successfully because of the respect, understanding, and trust he shown through active listening.

Alex also understood the value of mimicking and synchronizing nonverbal cues. They realized that building rapport and a connection with others required subtly matching their own body language, gestures, and even speaking patterns. Alex increased their power by giving their audience a sense of validation and understanding by imitating their nonverbal clues.

Alex noticed a significant improvement in their capacity to convince and influence people as they continued to hone their non-verbal communication skills. They understood that non-verbal clues may either support or contradict their vocal statements, altering the total impact of their communication. They also understood that words were only a part of the equation. With each encounter, Alex improved his awareness of the minute differences in non-verbal cues. They engaged in mindfulness exercises, paying attention to their own nonverbal signs, and persistently looking for feedback to improve their abilities. They accepted the notion that non-verbal persuasion was a dynamic ability that was constantly evolving. Alex considered the transforming impact of mastering non-verbal influence as Chapter 14 came to a close. They realized that they might establish a stronger connection with others, foster trust, and have a greater impact by mastering the subtleties of body language, facial expressions, voice clues, and active listening.

Alex looked ahead to the chapters that were ahead, determined to improve their non-verbal communication abilities. They understood that nonverbal communication was a crucial aspect of their journey, one that would develop through time and mould their capacity to effect lasting change.

Chapter 15
The Ever-Evolving Influence Journey

As Alex's journey of influence came to an end, the mentor shared with them the idea of accepting a lifetime of ongoing influence. They emphasized that influence was a lifelong path of growth, learning, and impact rather than a destination. The mentor provided examples of powerful people who had proven the power of lifelong impact in order to further discuss this subject. They talked about how these people had changed, evolved, and continually improved the lives of others. The mentor advised Alex to think of their ascendance to influence as a continuous process of growth and development.

Alex understood that in order to embrace a lifetime of ongoing influence, they needed to continue to be inquisitive and dedicated to learning. The mentor emphasized the value of maintaining an open mind, seeking out different viewpoints, and consistently developing one's knowledge and abilities. By doing this, Alex would be able to adapt to and remain relevant in a world that is changing quickly.

Alex first learned about thinking leadership from the mentor. They talked about how powerful people could influence debates, question the current quo, and present fresh approaches to important problems. They pushed Alex to develop into a thought leader in their sector, offering insightful commentary and igniting the imaginations of others. The mentor assisted Alex in creating a plan for personal development during their course. They pushed them to create a system for continual improvement and to set both short-term and long-term goals. In their drive to evolve into an influential person, Alex discovered the need of self-reflection, feedback, and continuous improvement.

The mentor also emphasized the need of networking and cooperation in sustaining influence. They talked about how powerful people forged ties, sought out partnerships, and collaborated to increase their influence. Alex discovered the importance of creating and maintaining a strong network of people with similar interests who might encourage and assist them on their continuing path to influence. As Chapter 15 went on, Alex came to terms with the notion that impact was not limited to a certain accomplishment or turning point. They were aware that their voyage represented a lifetime commitment to improving the lives of others. Alex experienced a sense of elation and purpose as they considered the limitless opportunities for ongoing influence.

The mentor reaffirmed to Alex that influence was not just determined by accolades or achievements received from others, but also by the long-lasting effects they had on people and society. They urged Alex to uphold their principles, be committed to their mission, and always act honorably. Alex would encourage others to follow them on the road of constant influence by doing so.

Alex was incredibly grateful for the advice and support they had received as the end of their influential journey drew near. They understood that their adventure had only just begun and that they had the ability to leave a lasting legacy of progress. Alex anxiously awaited the mentor's parting advice, ready to embrace a lifetime of ongoing influence with passion and purpose and their commitment to continuing learning, growth, and impact.

Chapter 16
The Ripple Impact

The mentor explained the profound idea of the ripple effect of influence to them as Alex's impactful journey reached its zenith. They emphasized that every choice, every action, and every word had the capacity to have an impact that went far beyond what was immediately seen. The mentor provided examples of influential people who had sparked a domino effect of good change in order to go deeper into this subject. They talked about how a single deed of kindness, an emotional exchange, or a game-changing notion may set off a chain of occasions that had a profound effect on many people's lives. The mentor urged Alex to understand the enormous potential for spreading influence.

Alex understood that their power extended beyond their contacts with one another and their immediate results. They were aware that their acts may encourage others to act, alter their viewpoints, and produce their own ripples of effect. The mentor advised Alex to think about the long-term effects they might have on people and communities, even after their own lives. The exercises the mentor led Alex through helped them recognize the numerous ways their influence may

materialize and have an impact. They investigated the use of social media to reach a wider audience and amplify their message, as well as the power of storytelling and public speaking. Alex started to realize that people's influence may reach far beyond their small social group and have an impact on those they may never meet.

The mentor emphasized the value of honesty & intentionality throughout the trainees' training to create a good ripple effect. They talked about how influential people were more likely to inspire others and spread their influence if they had a clear purpose and behaved in accordance with their principles. Alex discovered that others would be moved by their sincerity and real desire, which would inspire them to participate in bringing about change. The mentor also emphasized the value of teamwork and group action in enhancing the influence's ripple effect. They talked about how powerful people frequently teamed up with people who had similar ideals and objectives. Alex realized that by collaborating with like-minded people and groups, they might make a bigger effect and spark a chain reaction of progress.

Alex experienced a deep sense of exhilaration and responsibility as Chapter 16 developed. They were aware that their actions may have a domino impact on other people's lives, communities, and possibly the entire world. Alex pictured a time in the future when their deeds and decisions would encourage others to act as change agents, starting a wave of good impact that would spread and increase. The mentor emphasized to Alex that the process of influence's ripple effects was ongoing. They urged them to consider the effect they wished to have on others and to regularly assess the results of their activities. The mentor emphasized the ability of even seemingly insignificant acts of empathy, compassion, and kindness to have a profound impact on others and alter their direction in life.

Alex felt a deep sense of thankfulness for the life-changing experience they had experienced as their influential journey's concluding chapter drew near. They came to see that their rise to prominence was not the culmination of a lifelong dedication to bringing about constructive change. Alex anxiously awaited the mentor's parting advice as they were now aware of the ripple impact of influence and were prepared to move on with a clear sense of purpose, intention, and unwavering faith in the strength of their influence.

Author's Note:

Dear readers,

I hope you have enjoyed the engaging story-based trip through the chapters of "How to Win Hearts and Influence Minds." We have delved into the depths of influence throughout this book, examining its many sides and revealing its transformational potential. As we come to a close with this story, I want you to think about your own capacity for influence and how you might be able to use it to improve both your own life and the lives of others.

Keep in mind that influence is not just reserved for the powerful or the privileged few. Whether it be in our homes, communities, or the larger world, everyone of us has the power to affect change in our domains of influence. We are able to effect significant and long-lasting change when we work together.

I urge you to go off on your own influential trip while using the guidelines and wisdom offered throughout this book as your guide. Accept your distinctive strengths, value your authenticity, and uphold your commitment to lifelong learning. Like a pebble put into a pond, your influence may start off small, but it has the ability to spread far and wide.

Be mindful of the strength of compassion, empathy, and integrity as you move through the different chapters of your life. Look for opportunities to motivate, encourage, and assist others as they travel their own paths. To increase your effect, surround yourself with others who share your goal and are like-minded. Together, we can build a society that values each person's voice and thrives on constructive impact.

We appreciate your participation as we examine "The Art of Influencing." As you accept your own influential route, may it serve as a guidance and motivation for you. Keep in mind that you have the ability to influence the world and leave a lasting legacy of progress.

With sincere appreciation,

B.S.Rawat

Preeti Rawat

Glossary

The following list of terms from "How to Win Friends and Influence Minds" is accompanied by their definitions:

1. Influence: The capacity to influence or mould the ideas, opinions, deeds, or choices of others.

2. Art: The ability, method, or creative expression employed in the production of something significant or influential.

3. Impact: The result or effect of something on people, events, or consequences.

4. Transformation: A substantial and profound alteration or evolution of oneself or of a circumstance.

5. Authenticity: Being truthful, true, and true to oneself in one's thoughts, deeds, and dealings with others.

6. Empathy: The capacity to comprehend and empathies with the thoughts, feelings, and experiences of another.

7. Communication: It is the vocal, nonverbal, or written process of conveying information, ideas, or emotions.

8. Persuasion: The process of persuading or influencing someone else to adopt a particular belief, carry out a particular action, or alter their point of view.

9. Leadership: The capacity to motivate, lead, and sway people towards a single objective or vision.

10. Ethics: Moral guidelines and values that direct conduct and judgment in order to uphold justice, honesty, and integrity.

11. Power: The capacity to exercise power, influence, or control over another person or circumstance.

12. Connection: Building trusting connections, promoting mutual understanding, and forging links with people.

13. Empowerment is the process of enabling and assisting people in realizing their full potential, making choices, and acting.

14. Change: The act of changing a situation, circumstance, or point of view.

15. Self-awareness: Being fully aware of one's own ideas, feelings, abilities, limitations, and values.

16. Integrity: Adhering to one's values, morals, and ethical guidelines.

17. Collaboration: It is the process of working with others to achieve a common objective while utilizing a variety of viewpoints and skills.

18. Mindfulness: Being fully alert to one's surroundings, thoughts, and feelings at all times.

19. Adaptability: The capacity to modify or respond successfully to alterations, difficulties, or novel situations.

20. Resilience: The ability to recover, adapt, or bounce back in the face of difficulties, setbacks, or adversity.

21. Trust: An acceptance of the competence, dependability, and honesty of others, which promotes collaboration and teamwork.

22. Influence tactics: Particular approaches or procedures used to influence, persuade, or convince others.

23. The capacity to identify, comprehend, and control one's own emotions as well as those of others.

24. Active and attentive listening skills: The capacity to comprehend and translate both verbal and nonverbal information.

25. Storytelling: It is the art of using a narrative or story to convey a message, a concept, or an experience.

26. Networking: Creating and maintaining connections with others for influence, cooperation, and support.

27. Influence in the digital age: The use of influence strategies and techniques in the context of technology, social media, and digital communication platforms is known as "influence in the digital age".

28. Positive Psychology: It emphasizes strengths and positive facets of human functioning, is the study of psychological well-being, happiness, and thriving.

29. Motivation: The internal or external forces that propel people to act, seek objectives, or realize desired results.

30. Negotiation: The process of coming to a compromise or conclusion through dialogue.

Ingram Content Group UK Ltd.
Milton Keynes UK
UKHW010738170723
425272UK00004B/149